UNITY OF GOOD

BY

MARY BAKER EDDY

AUTHOR OF SCIENCE AND HEALTH WITH KEY TO
THE SCRIPTURES

Originally published in 1887.

Contents

Personal Statements

Credo

Do you believe in God?

Do you believe in man?

Do you believe in matter?

What say you of woman?

What say you of evil?

Suffering from Others' Thoughts

The Saviour's Mission

Summary

Caution in the Truth

Perhaps no doctrine of Christian Science rouses so much natural doubt and questioning as this, that God knows no such thing as sin. Indeed, this may be set down as one of the "things hard to be understood," such as the apostle Peter declared were taught by his fellow-apostle Paul, "which they that are unlearned and unstable wrest ... unto their own destruction." (2 Peter iii. 16.)

Let us then reason together on this important subject, whose statement in Christian Science may justly be characterized as wonderful.

Does God know or behold sin, sickness, and death?

The nature and character of God is so little apprehended and demonstrated by mortals, that I counsel my students to defer this infinite inquiry, in their discussions of Christian Science. In fact, they had better leave the subject untouched, until they draw nearer to the divine character, and are practically able to testify, by their lives, that as they *ACIM* come closer to the true understanding of God they lose all sense of error.

The Scriptures declare that God is too pure to behold iniquity (Habakkuk i. 13); but they also declare that God *there* pitieth them who fear Him; that there is no place where His *you* voice is not heard; that He is "a very present help in *go.* trouble."

The sinner has no refuge from sin, except in God, who is his salvation. We must, however, realize God's presence, *We can...* power, and love, in order to be saved from sin. This *realize God's presence.*

(not big on "must")

realization takes away man's fondness for sin and his pleasure in it; and, lastly, it removes the pain which accrues to him from it. Then follows this, as the finale in Science: The sinner loses his sense of sin, and gains a higher sense of God, in whom there is no sin.

I sin because I'm lonely

The true man, really saved, is ready to testify of God in the infinite penetration of Truth, and can affirm that the Mind which is good, or God, has no knowledge of sin.

yes

In the same manner the sick lose their sense of sickness, and gain that spiritual sense of harmony which contains neither discord nor disease.

disease = mind smell — m. error in thought

when
According to this same rule, in divine Science, the dying—if they die in the Lord—awake from a sense of death to a sense of Life in Christ, with a knowledge of Truth and Love beyond what they possessed before; because their lives have grown so far toward the stature of manhood in Christ Jesus, that they are ready for a spiritual transfiguration, through their affections and understanding.

we all drew the Lord. God is not a club.

God.

Those who reach this transition, called death, without having rightly improved the lessons of this primary school of mortal existence,—and still believe in matter's reality, pleasure, and pain,—are not ready to understand immortality. Hence they awake only to another sphere of experience, and must pass through another probationary state before it can be truly said of them: "Blessed are the dead which die in the Lord."

hmmm not sure of this

God.

They upon whom the second death, of which we read in the Apocalypse (Revelation xx. 6), hath no power, are those who have obeyed God's commands, and have washed their robes white through the sufferings of the flesh and the triumphs of Spirit. Thus they have reached the goal in divine Science, by knowing Him in whom they have believed. This knowledge is not the forbidden fruit of sin, sickness, and death, but it is the fruit which grows on the "tree of life." This is the understanding of God, whereby man is found in the image and likeness of good, not of evil; of health, not of sickness; of Life, not of death.

God is All-in-all. Hence He is in Himself only, in His own nature and character, and is perfect being, or consciousness. He is all the Life and Mind there is or can be. Within Himself is every embodiment of Life and Mind.

If He is All, He can have no consciousness of anything unlike Himself; because, if He is omnipresent, there can be nothing outside of Himself.

Now this self-same God is our helper. He pities us. He has mercy upon us, and guides every event of our careers. He is near to them who adore Him. To understand Him, without a single taint of our mortal, finite sense of sin, sickness, or death, is to approach Him and become like Him.

Truth is God, and in God's law. This law declares that Truth is All, and there is no error. This law of Truth destroys every phase of error. To gain a temporary consciousness of God's law is to feel, in a certain finite human sense, that God comes to us and pities us; but the attainment of the understanding of His presence, through the Science of God, destroys our sense of imperfection, or of His absence, through a diviner sense that God is all true consciousness; and this convinces us that, as we get still nearer Him, we must forever lose our own consciousness of error.

But how could we lose all consciousness of error, if God be conscious of it? God has not forbidden man to know Him; on the contrary, the Father bids man have the same Mind "which was also in Christ Jesus,"—which was certainly the divine Mind; but God does forbid man's acquaintance with evil. Why? Because evil is no part of the divine knowledge.

John's Gospel declares (xvii. 3) that "life eternal" consists in the knowledge of the only true God, and of Jesus Christ, whom He has sent. Surely from such an understanding of Science, such knowing, the vision of sin is wholly excluded.

Nevertheless, at the present crude hour, no wise men or women will rudely or prematurely agitate a theme involving the All of infinity.

Rather will they rejoice in the small understanding they have already gained of the wholeness of Deity, and work gradually and gently up toward the perfect thought divine. This meekness will increase their apprehension of God, because their mental struggles and pride of opinion will proportionately diminish.

Every one should be encouraged not to accept any personal opinion on so great a matter, but to seek the divine Science of this question of Truth by following upward individual convictions, undisturbed by the frightened sense of any need of attempting to solve every Life-problem in a day.

"Great is the mystery of godliness," says Paul; and mystery involves the unknown. No stubborn purpose to force conclusions on this subject will unfold in us a higher sense of Deity; neither will it promote the Cause of Truth or enlighten the individual thought.

Let us respect the rights of conscience and the liberty of the sons of God, so letting our "moderation be known to all men." Let no enmity, no untempered controversy, spring up between Christian Science students and Christians who wholly or partially differ from them as to the nature of sin and the marvellous unity of man with God shadowed forth in scientific thought. Rather let the stately goings of this wonderful part of Truth be left to the supernal guidance.

"These are but parts of Thy ways," says Job; and the whole is greater than its parts. Our present understanding is but "the seed within itself," for it is divine Science, "bearing fruit after its kind."

Sooner or later the whole human race will learn that, in proportion as the spotless selfhood of God is understood, human nature will be renovated, and man will receive a higher selfhood, derived from God, and the redemption of mortals from sin, sickness, and death be established on everlasting foundations.

The Science of physical harmony, as now presented to the people in divine light, is radical enough to promote as forcible collisions of thought as the age has strength to bear. Until the heavenly law of health, according to Christian Science, is firmly grounded, even the thinkers are not prepared to answer intelligently leading questions about God and sin, and the world is far from ready to assimilate such a grand and all-absorbing verity concerning the divine nature and character as is embraced in the theory of God's blindness to error and ignorance of sin. No wise mother, though a graduate of Wellesley College, will talk to her babe about the problems of Euclid.

Not much more than a half-century ago the assertion of universal salvation provoked discussion and horror, similar to what our declarations about sin and Deity must arouse, if hastily pushed to the front while the platoons of Christian Science are not yet thoroughly drilled in the plainer manual of their spiritual armament. "Wait patiently on the Lord;" and in less than another fifty years His name will be magnified in the apprehension of this new subject, as already He is glorified in the wide extension of belief in the impartial grace of God,—shown by the changes at Andover Seminary and in multitudes of other religious folds.

Nevertheless, though I thus speak, and from my heart of hearts, it is due both to Christian Science and myself to make also the following statement: When I have most clearly seen and most sensibly felt that the infinite recognizes no disease, this has not separated me from God, but has so bound me to Him as to enable me instantaneously to heal a cancer which had eaten its way to the jugular vein.

In the same spiritual condition I have been able to replace dislocated joints and raise the dying to instantaneous health. People are now living who can bear witness to these cures. Herein is my evidence, from on high, that the views here promulgated on this subject are correct.

Certain self-proved propositions pour into my waiting thought in connection with these experiences; and here is one such conviction: that an acknowledgment of the perfection of the infinite Unseen confers a power nothing else can. An incontestable point in divine Science is, that because God is All, a realization of this fact dispels even the sense or consciousness of sin, and brings us nearer to God, bringing out the highest phenomena of the All-Mind.

Seedtime and Harvest

Let another query now be considered, which gives much trouble to many earnest thinkers before Science answers it.

Is anything real of which the physical senses are cognizant?

Everything is as real as you make it, and no more so. What you see, hear, feel, is a mode of consciousness, and can have no other reality than the sense you entertain of it.

It is dangerous to rest upon the evidence of the senses, for this evidence is not absolute, and therefore not real, in our sense of the word. All that is beautiful and good in your individual consciousness is permanent. That which is not so is illusive and fading. My insistence upon a proper understanding of the unreality of matter and evil arises from their deleterious effects, physical, moral, and intellectual, upon the race.

All forms of error are uprooted in Science, on the same basis whereby sickness is healed,—namely, by the establishment, through reason, revelation, and Science, of the nothingness of every claim of error, even the doctrine of heredity and other physical causes. You demonstrate the process of Science, and it proves my view conclusively, that mortal mind is the cause of all disease. Destroy the mental sense of the disease, and the disease itself disappears. Destroy the sense of sin, and sin itself disappears.

Material and sensual consciousness are mortal. Hence they must, some time and in some way, be reckoned unreal. That time has partially come, or my words would not have been spoken. Jesus has made the way plain,—so plain that all are without excuse who walk not in it; but this way is not the path of physical science, human philosophy, or mystic psychology.

The talent and genius of the centuries have wrongly reckoned. They have not based upon revelation their arguments and conclusions as to the source and resources of being,—its combinations, phenomena, and outcome,— but have built instead upon the sand of human reason. They have not accepted the simple teaching and life of Jesus as the only true solution of the perplexing problem of human existence.

Sometimes it is said, by those who fail to understand me, that I monopolize; and this is said because ideas akin to mine have been held by a few spiritual thinkers in all ages. So they have, but in a far different form. Healing has gone on continually; yet healing, as I teach it, has not been practised since the days of Christ.

What is the cardinal point of the difference in my metaphysical system? This: that by knowing the unreality of disease, sin, and death, you demonstrate the allness of God. This difference wholly separates my system from all others. The reality of these so-called existences I deny, because they are not to be found in God, and this system is built on Him as the sole cause. It would be difficult to name any previous teachers, save Jesus and his apostles, who have thus taught.

If there be any monopoly in my teaching, it lies in this utter reliance upon the one God, to whom belong all things,

Life is God, or Spirit, the supersensible eternal. The universe and man are the spiritual phenomena of this one infinite Mind. Spiritual phenomena never converge toward aught but infinite Deity. Their gradations are spiritual and divine; they cannot collapse, or lapse into their opposites, for God is their divine Principle. They live, because He lives; and they are eternally perfect, because He is perfect, and governs them in the Truth of divine Science, whereof God is the Alpha and Omega, the centre and circumference.

To attempt the calculation of His mighty ways, from the evidence before the material senses, is fatuous. It is like commencing with the minus sign, to learn the principle of positive mathematics.

God was not in the whirlwind. He is not the blind force of a material universe. Mortals must learn this; unless, pursued by their fears, they would endeavor to hide from His presence under their own falsities, and call in vain for the mountains of unholiness to shield them from the penalty of error.

Jesus taught us to walk over, not into or with, the currents of matter, or mortal mind. His teachings beard the lions in their dens. He turned the water into wine, he commanded the winds, he healed the sick,—all in direct opposition to human philosophy and so-called natural science. He annulled the laws of matter, showing them to be laws of mortal mind, not of God. He showed the need of changing this mind and its abortive laws. He demanded a change of consciousness and evidence, and effected this change through the higher laws of God. The palsied hand moved, despite the boastful sense of physical law and order. Jesus stooped not to human consciousness, nor to the evidence of the senses. He heeded not the taunt, "That withered hand looks very real and feels very real;" but he cut off this vain boasting and destroyed human pride by taking away the material evidence. If his patient was a theologian of some bigoted sect, a physician, or a professor of natural philosophy,—according to the ruder sort then prevalent,— he never thanked Jesus for restoring his senseless hand; but neither red tape nor indignity hindered the divine process. Jesus required neither cycles of time nor thought in order to mature fitness for perfection and its possibilities. He said that the kingdom of heaven is here, and is included in Mind; that while ye say, There are yet four months, and then cometh the harvest, I say, Look up, not down, for your fields are already white for the harvest; and gather the harvest by mental, not material processes. The laborers are few in this vineyard of Mind-sowing and reaping; but let them apply to the waiting grain the curving sickle of Mind's eternal circle, and bind it with bands of Soul.

The Deep Things of God

Science reverses the evidence of the senses in theology, on the same principle that it does in astronomy. Popular theology makes God tributary to man, coming at human call; whereas the reverse is true in Science. Men must approach God reverently, doing their own work in obedience to divine law, if they would fulfil the intended harmony of being.

The principle of music knows nothing of discord. God is harmony's selfhood. His universal laws, His unchangeableness, are not infringed in ethics any more than in music. To Him there is no moral inharmony; as we shall learn, proportionately as we gain the true understanding of Deity. If God could be conscious of sin, His infinite power would straightway reduce the universe to chaos.

If God has any real knowledge of sin, sickness, and death, they must be eternal; since He is, in the very fibre of His being, "without beginning of years or end of days." If God knows that which is not permanent, it follows that He knows something which He must learn to unknow, for the benefit of our race.

Such a view would bring us upon an outworn theological platform, which contains such planks as the divine repentance, and the belief that God must one day do His work over again, because it was not at first done aright.

Can it be seriously held, by any thinker, that long after God made the universe,—earth, man, animals, plants, the sun, the moon, and "the stars also,"—He should so gain wisdom and power from past experience that He could vastly improve upon His own previous work,—as Burgess, the boatbuilder, remedies in the Volunteer the shortcomings of the Puritan's model?

Christians are commanded to grow in grace. Was it necessary for God to grow in grace, that He might rectify His spiritual universe?

The Jehovah of limited Hebrew faith might need repentance, because His created children proved sinful; but the New Testament tells us of "the Father of lights, with whom is no variableness, neither shadow of turning." God is not the shifting vane on the spire, but the corner-stone of living rock, firmer than everlasting hills.

As God is Mind, if this Mind is familiar with evil, all cannot be good therein. Our infinite model would be taken away. What is in eternal Mind must be reflected in man, Mind's image. How then could man escape, or hope to escape, from a knowledge which is everlasting in his creator?

God never said that man would become better by learning to distinguish evil from good,—but the contrary, that by this knowledge, by man's first disobedience, came "death into the world, and all our woe."

"Shall mortal man be more just than God?" asks the poet-patriarch. May men rid themselves of an incubus which God never can throw off? Do mortals know more than God, that they may declare Him absolutely cognizant of sin?

God created all things, and pronounced them good. Was evil among these good things? Man is God's child and image. If God knows evil, so must man, or the likeness is incomplete, the image marred.

If man must be destroyed by the knowledge of evil, then his destruction comes through the very knowledge caught from God, and the creature is punished for his likeness to his creator.

God is commonly called the sinless, and man the sinful; but if the thought of sin could be possible in Deity, would Deity then be sinless? Would God not of necessity take precedence as the infinite sinner, and human sin become only an echo of the divine?

Such vagaries are to be found in heathen religious history. There are, or have been, devotees who worship not the good Deity, who will not harm them, but the bad deity, who seeks to do them mischief, and whom therefore they wish to bribe with prayers into quiescence, as a criminal appeases, with a money-bag, the venal officer.

Surely this is no Christian worship! In Christianity man bows to the infinite perfection which he is bidden to imitate. In Truth, such terms as divine sin and infinite sinner are unheard-of contradictions,—absurdities; but would they be sheer nonsense, if God has, or can have, a real knowledge of sin?

Ways Higher than Our Ways

A lie has only one chance of successful deception,—to be accounted true. Evil seeks to fasten all error upon God, and so make the lie seem part of eternal Truth.

Emerson says, "Hitch your wagon to a star." I say, Be allied to the deific power, and all that is good will aid your journey, as the stars in their courses fought against Sisera. (Judges v. 20.) Hourly, in Christian Science, man thus weds himself with God, or rather he ratifies a union predestined from all eternity; but evil ties its wagon-load of offal to the divine chariots,—or seeks so to do,—that its vileness may be christened purity, and its darkness get consolation from borrowed scintillations.

Jesus distinctly taught the arrogant Pharisees that, from the beginning, their father, the devil, was the would-be murderer of Truth. A right apprehension of the wonderful utterances of him who "spake as never man spake," would despoil error of its borrowed plumes, and transform the universe into a home of marvellous light,—"a consummation devoutly to be wished."

Error says God must know evil because He knows all things; but Holy Writ declares God told our first parents that in the day when they should partake of the fruit of evil, they must surely die. Would it not absurdly follow that God must perish, if He knows evil and evil necessarily leads to extinction? Rather let us think of God as saying, I am infinite good; therefore I know not evil. Dwelling in light, I can see only the brightness of My own glory.

Error may say that God can never save man from sin, if He knows and sees it not; but God says, I am too pure to behold iniquity, and destroy everything that is unlike Myself.

Many fancy that our heavenly Father reasons thus: If pain and sorrow were not in My mind, I could not remedy them, and wipe the tears from the eyes of My children. Error says you must know grief in order to console it. Truth, God, says you oftenest console others in troubles that you have not. Is not our comforter always from outside and above ourselves?

God says, I show My pity through divine law, not through human. It is My sympathy with and My knowledge of harmony (not inharmony) which alone enable Me to rebuke, and eventually destroy, every supposition of discord.

Error says God must know death in order to strike at its root; but God saith, I am ever-conscious Life, and thus I conquer death; for to be ever conscious of Life is to be never conscious of death. I am All. A knowledge of aught beside Myself is impossible.

If such knowledge of evil were possible to God, it would lower His rank.

With God, knowledge is necessarily foreknowledge; and foreknowledge and foreordination must be one, in an infinite Being. What Deity foreknows, Deity must foreordain; else He is not omnipotent, and, like ourselves, He foresees events which are contrary to His creative will, yet which He cannot avert.

If God knows evil at all, He must have had foreknowledge thereof; and if He foreknew it, He must virtually have intended it, or ordered it aforetime,—foreordained it; else how could it have come into the world?

But this we cannot believe of God; for if the supreme good could predestine or foreknow evil, there would be sin in Deity, and this would be the end of infinite moral unity. "If therefore the light that is in thee be darkness, how great is that darkness!" On the contrary, evil is only a delusive deception, without any actuality which Truth can know.

Rectifications

How is a mistake to be rectified? By reversal or revision,— by seeing it in its proper light, and then turning it or turning from it.

We undo the statements of error by reversing them.

Through these three statements, or misstatements, evil comes into authority:—

First: The Lord created it.

Second: The Lord knows it.

Third: I am afraid of it.

By a reverse process of argument evil must be dethroned:—

First: God never made evil.

Second: He knows it not.

Third: We therefore need not fear it.

Try this process, dear inquirer, and so reach that perfect Love which "casteth out fear," and then see if this Love does not destroy in you all hate and the sense of evil. You will awake to the perception of God as All-in-all. You will find yourself losing the knowledge and the operation of sin, proportionably as you realize the divine infinitude and believe that He can see nothing outside of His own focal distance.

A Colloquy

In Romans (ii. 15) we read the apostle's description of mental processes wherein human thoughts are "the mean while accusing or else excusing one another." If we observe our mental processes, we shall find that we are perpetually arguing with ourselves; yet each mortal is not two personalities, but one.

In like manner good and evil talk to one another; yet they are not two but one, for evil is naught, and good only is reality.

Evil. God hath said, "Ye shall eat of every tree of the garden." If you do not, your intellect will be circumscribed and the evidence of your personal senses be denied. This would antagonize individual consciousness and existence.

Good. The Lord is God. With Him is no consciousness of evil, because there is nothing beside Him or outside of Him. Individual consciousness in man is inseparable from good. There is no sensible matter, no sense in matter; but there is a spiritual sense, a sense of Spirit, and this is the only consciousness belonging to true individuality, or a divine sense of being.

Evil. Why is this so?

Good. Because man is made after God's eternal likeness, and this likeness consists in a sense of harmony and immortality, in which no evil can possibly dwell. You may eat of the fruit of Godlikeness, but as to the fruit of ungodliness, which is opposed to Truth,—ye shall not touch it, lest ye die.

Evil. But I would taste and know error for myself.

Good. Thou shalt not admit that error is something to know or be known, to eat or be eaten, to see or be seen, to feel or be felt. To admit the existence of error would be to admit the truth of a lie.

Evil. But there is something besides good. God knows that a knowledge of this something is essential to happiness and life. A lie is as genuine as Truth, though not so legitimate a child of God. Whatever exists must come from God, and be important to our knowledge. Error, even, is His offspring.

Good. Whatever cometh not from the eternal Spirit, has its origin in the physical senses and material brains, called human intellect and will-power,—alias intelligent matter.

In Shakespeare's tragedy of King Lear, it was the traitorous and cruel treatment received by old Gloster from his bastard son Edmund which makes true the lines:

The gods are just, and of our pleasant vices

Make instruments to scourge us.

His lawful son, Edgar, was to his father ever loyal. Now God has no bastards to turn again and rend their Maker. The divine children are born of law and order, and Truth knows only such.

How well the Shakespearean tale agrees with the word of Scripture, in Hebrews xii. 7, 8: "If ye endure chastening, God dealeth with you as with sons; for what son is he whom the father chasteneth not? But if ye be without chastisement, whereof all are partakers, then are ye bastards, and not sons."

The doubtful or spurious evidence of the senses is not to be admitted,—especially when they testify concerning Spirit, whereof they are confessedly incompetent to speak.

Evil. But mortal mind and sin really exist!

Good. How can they exist, unless God has created them? And how can He create anything so wholly unlike Himself and foreign to His nature? An evil material mind, so-called, can conceive of God only as like itself, and knowing both evil and good; but a purely good and spiritual consciousness has no sense whereby to cognize evil. Mortal mind is the opposite of immortal Mind, and sin the opposite of goodness. I am the infinite All. From me proceedeth all Mind, all consciousness, all individuality, all being. My Mind is divine good, and cannot drift into evil. To believe in minds many is to depart from the supreme sense of harmony. Your assumptions insist that there is more than the one Mind, more than the one God; but verily I say unto you, God is All-in-all; and you can never be outside of His oneness.

Evil. I am a finite consciousness, a material individuality,—a mind in matter, which is both evil and good.

Good. All consciousness is Mind; and Mind is God,—an infinite, and not a finite consciousness. This consciousness is reflected in individual consciousness, or man, whose source is infinite Mind. There is no really finite mind, no finite consciousness. There is no material substance, for Spirit is all that endureth, and hence is the only substance. There is, can be, no evil mind, because Mind is God. God and His ideas—that is, God and the universe—constitute all that exists. Man, as God's offspring, must be spiritual, perfect, eternal.

Evil. I am something separate from good or God. I am substance. My mind is more than matter. In my mortal mind, matter becomes conscious, and is able to see, taste, hear, feel, smell. Whatever matter thus affirms is mainly correct. If you, O good, deny this, then I deny your truthfulness. If you say that matter is unconscious, you stultify my intellect, insult my conscience, and dispute self-evident facts; for nothing can be clearer than the testimony of the five senses.

Good. Spirit is the only substance. Spirit is God, and God is good; hence good is the only substance, the only Mind. Mind is not, cannot be, in matter. It sees, hears, feels, tastes, smells as Mind, and not as matter. Matter cannot talk; and hence, whatever it appears to say of itself is a lie. This lie, that Mind can be in matter,—claiming to be something beside God, denying Truth and its demonstration in Christian Science,—this lie I declare an illusion. This denial enlarges the human intellect by removing its evidence from sense to Soul, and from finiteness into infinity. It honors conscious human individuality by showing God as its source.

Evil. I am a creator,—but upon a material, not a spiritual basis. I give life, and I can destroy life.

Good. Evil is not a creator. God, good, is the only creator. Evil is not conscious or conscientious Mind; it is not individual, not actual. Evil is not spiritual, and therefore has no groundwork in Life, whose only source is Spirit. The elements which belong to the eternal All,—Life, Truth, Love,—evil can never take away.

Evil. I am intelligent matter; and matter is egoistic, having its own innate selfhood and the capacity to evolve mind. God is in matter, and matter reproduces God. From Him come my forms, near or remote. This is my honor, that God is my author, authority, governor, disposer. I am proud to be in His outstretched hands, and I shirk all responsibility for myself as evil, and for my varying manifestations.

Good. You mistake, O evil! God is not your authority and law. Neither is He the author of the material changes, the phantasma, a belief in which leads to such teaching as we find in the hymn-verse so often sung in church:—

Chance and change are busy ever,

Man decays and ages move;

But His mercy waneth never,—

God is wisdom, God is love.

Now if it be true that God's power never waneth, how can it be also true that chance and change are universal factors,—that man decays? Many ordinary Christians protest against this stanza of Bowring's, and its sentiment is foreign to Christian Science. If God be changeless goodness, as sings another line of this hymn, what place has chance in the divine economy? Nay, there is in God naught fantastic. All is real, all is serious. The phantasmagoria is a product of human dreams.

The Ego

From various friends comes inquiry as to the meaning of a word employed in the foregoing colloquy.

There are two English words, often used as if they were synonyms, which really have a shade of difference between them.

An egotist is one who talks much of himself. Egotism implies vanity and self-conceit.

Egoism is a more philosophical word, signifying a passionate love of self, which doubts all existence except its own. An egoist, therefore, is one uncertain of everything except his own existence.

Applying these distinctions to evil and God, we shall find that evil is egotistic,—boastful, but fleeing like a shadow at daybreak; while God is egoistic, knowing only His own all-presence, all-knowledge, all-power. *huh — ? there's nothing about "I" about God.*

Oh wait — w/ Moses — "I am that I am" — huh.

Soul

We read in the Hebrew Scriptures, "The soul that sinneth, it shall die."

What is Soul? Is it a reality within the mortal body? Who can prove that? Anatomy has not descried nor described Soul. It was never touched by the scalpel nor cut with the dissecting-knife. The five physical senses do not cognize it.

Who, then, dares define Soul as something within man? As well might you declare some old castle to be peopled with demons or angels, though never a light or form was discerned therein, and not a spectre had ever been seen going in or coming out.

The common hypotheses about souls are even more vague than ordinary material conjectures, and have less basis; because material theories are built on the evidence of the material senses.

Soul must be God; since we learn Soul only as we learn God, by spiritualization. As the five senses take no cognizance of Soul, so they take no cognizance of God. Whatever cannot be taken in by mortal mind—by human reflection, reason, or belief—must be the unfathomable

Mind, which "eye hath not seen, nor ear heard." Soul stands in this relation to every hypothesis as to its human character.

If Soul sins, it is a sinner, and Jewish law condemned the sinner to death,—as does all criminal law, to a certain extent.

Spirit never sins, because Spirit is God. Hence, as Spirit, Soul is sinless, and is God. Therefore there is, there can be, no spiritual death.

Transcending the evidence of the material senses, Science declares God to be the Soul of all being, the only Mind and intelligence in the universe. There is but one God, one Soul, or Mind, and that one is infinite, supplying all that is absolutely immutable and eternal,—Truth, Life, Love.

Science reveals Soul as that which the senses cannot define from any standpoint of their own. What the physical senses miscall soul, Christian Science defines as material sense; and herein lies the discrepancy between the true Science of Soul and that material sense of a soul which that very sense declares can never be seen or measured or weighed or touched by physicality.

Often we can elucidate the deep meaning of the Scriptures by reading sense instead of soul, as in the Forty-second Psalm: "Why art thou cast down, O my soul [sense]?... Hope thou in God [Soul]: for I shall yet praise Him, who is the health of my countenance, and my God [my Soul, immortality]."

The Virgin-mother's sense being uplifted to behold Spirit as the sole origin of man, she exclaimed, "My soul [spiritual sense] doth magnify the Lord."

Human language constantly uses the word soul for sense. This it does under the delusion that the senses can reverse the spiritual facts of Science, whereas Science reverses the testimony of the material senses.

Soul is Life, and being spiritual Life, never sins. Material sense is the so-called material life. Hence this lower sense sins and suffers, according to material belief, till divine understanding takes away this belief and restores Soul, or spiritual Life. "He restoreth my soul," says David.

In his first epistle to the Corinthians (xv. 45) Paul writes: "The first man Adam was made a living soul; the last Adam was made a quickening spirit." The apostle refers to the second Adam as the Messiah, our blessed Master, whose interpretation of God and His creation—by restoring the spiritual sense of man as immortal instead of mortal—made humanity victorious over death and the grave.

When I discovered the power of Spirit to break the cords of matter, through a change in the mortal sense of things, then I discerned the last Adam as a quickening Spirit, and understood the meaning of the declaration of Holy Writ, "The first shall be last,"—the living Soul shall be found a quickening Spirit; or, rather, shall reflect the Life of the divine Arbiter.

There is no Matter

"God is a Spirit" (or, more accurately translated, "God is Spirit"), declares the Scripture (John iv. 24), "and they that worship Him must worship Him in spirit and in truth."

If God is Spirit, and God is All, surely there can be no matter; for the divine All must be Spirit.

The tendency of Christianity is to spiritualize thought and action. The demonstrations of Jesus annulled the claims of matter, and overruled laws material as emphatically as they annihilated sin.

According to Christian Science, the first idolatrous claim of sin is, that matter exists; the second, that matter is substance; the third, that matter has intelligence; and the fourth, that matter, being so endowed, produces life and death.

Hence my conscientious position, in the denial of matter, rests on the fact that matter usurps the authority of God, Spirit; and the nature and character of matter, the antipode of Spirit, include all that denies and defies Spirit, in quantity or quality.

This subject can be enlarged. It can be shown, in detail, that evil does not obtain in Spirit, God; and that God, or good, is Spirit alone; whereas, evil does, according to belief, obtain in matter; and that evil is a false claim,—false to God, false to Truth and Life. Hence the claim of matter usurps the prerogative of God, saying, "I am a creator. God made me, and I make man and the material universe."

Spirit is the only creator, and man, including the universe, is His spiritual concept. By matter is commonly meant mind,—not the highest Mind, but a false form of mind. This so-called mind and matter cannot be separated in origin and action.

What is this mind? It is not the Mind of Spirit; for spiritualization of thought destroys all sense of matter as substance, Life, or intelligence, and enthrones God in the eternal qualities of His being.

This lower, misnamed mind is a false claim, a suppositional mind, which I prefer to call mortal mind. True Mind is immortal. This mortal mind declares itself material, in sin, sickness, and death, virtually saying, "I am the opposite of Spirit, of holiness, harmony, and Life."

To this declaration Christian Science responds, even as did our Master: "You were a murderer from the beginning. The truth abode not in you. You are a liar, and the father of it." Here it appears that a liar was in the neuter gender,— neither masculine nor feminine. Hence it was not man (the image of God) who lied, but the false claim to personality, which I call mortal mind; a claim which Christian Science uncovers, in order to demonstrate the falsity of the claim.

There are lesser arguments which prove matter to be identical with mortal mind, and this mind a lie.

The physical senses (matter really having no sense) give the only pretended testimony there can be as to the existence of a substance called matter. Now these senses, being material, can only testify from their own evidence, and concerning themselves; yet we have it on divine authority: "If I bear witness of myself, my witness is not true." (John v. 31.)

In other words: matter testifies of itself, "I am matter;" but unless matter is mind, it cannot talk or testify; and if it is mind, it is certainly not the Mind of Christ, not the Mind that is identical with Truth.

Brain, thus assuming to testify, is only matter within the skull, and is believed to be mind only through error and delusion. Examine that form of matter called brains, and you find no mind therein. Hence the logical sequence, that there is in reality neither matter nor mortal mind, but that the self-testimony of the physical senses is false.

Examine these witnesses for error, or falsity, and observe the foundations of their testimony, and you will find them divided in evidence, mocking the Scripture (Matthew xviii. 16), "In the mouth of two or three witnesses every word may be established."

Sight. Mortal mind declares that matter sees through the organizations of matter, or that mind sees by means of matter. Disorganize the so-called material structure, and then mortal mind says, "I cannot see;" and declares that matter is the master of mind, and that non-intelligence governs. Mortal mind admits that it sees only material images, pictured on the eye's retina.

What then is the line of the syllogism? It must be this: That matter is not seen; that mortal mind cannot see without matter; and therefore that the whole function of material sight is an illusion, a lie.

Here comes in the summary of the whole matter, wherewith we started: that God is All, and God is Spirit; therefore there is nothing but Spirit; and consequently there is no matter.

Touch. Take another train of reasoning. Mortal mind says that matter cannot feel matter; yet put your finger on a burning coal, and the nerves, material nerves, do feel matter.

Again I ask: What evidence does mortal mind afford that matter is substantial, is hot or cold? Take away mortal mind, and matter could not feel what it calls substance. Take away matter, and mortal mind could not cognize its own so-called substance, and this so-called mind would have no identity. Nothing would remain to be seen or felt.

What is substance? What is the reality of God and the universe? Immortal Mind is the real substance,—Spirit, Life, Truth, and Love.

Taste. Mortal mind says, "I taste; and this is sweet, this is sour." Let mortal mind change, and say that sour is sweet, and so it would be. If every mortal mind believed sweet to be sour, it would be so; for the qualities of matter are but qualities of mortal mind. Change the mind, and the quality changes. Destroy the belief, and the quality disappears.

The so-called material senses are found, upon examination, to be mortally mental, instead of material. Reduced to its proper denomination, matter is mortal mind; yet, strictly speaking, there is no mortal mind, for Mind is immortal, and is not matter, but Spirit.

Force. What is gravitation? Mortal mind says gravitation is a material power, or force. I ask, Which was first, matter or power? That which was first was God, immortal Mind, the Parent of all. But God is Truth, and the forces of Truth are moral and spiritual, not physical. They are not the merciless forces of matter. What then are the so-called forces of matter? They are the phenomena of mortal mind, and matter and mortal mind are one; and this one is a misstatement of Mind, God.

A molecule, as matter, is not formed by Spirit; for Spirit is spiritual consciousness alone. Hence this spiritual consciousness can form nothing unlike itself, Spirit, and Spirit is the only creator. The material atom is an outlined falsity of consciousness, which can gather additional evidence of consciousness and life only as it adds lie to lie. This process it names material attraction, and endows with the double capacity of creator and creation.

From the beginning this lie was the false witness against the fact that Spirit is All, beside which there is no other existence. The use of a lie is that it unwittingly confirms Truth, when handled by Christian Science, which reverses false testimony and gains a knowledge of God from opposite facts, or phenomena.

This whole subject is met and solved by Christian Science according to Scripture. Thus we see that Spirit is Truth and eternal reality; that matter is the opposite of Spirit,— referred to in the New Testament as the flesh at war with Spirit; hence, that matter is erroneous, transitory, unreal.

A further proof of this is the demonstration, according to Christian Science, that by the reduction and the rejection of the claims of matter (instead of acquiescence therein) man is improved physically, mentally, morally, spiritually.

To deny the existence or reality of matter, and yet admit the reality of moral evil, sin, or to say that the divine Mind is conscious of evil, yet is not conscious of matter, is erroneous. This error stultifies the logic of divine Science, and must interfere with its practical demonstration.

Is There no Death?

Jesus not only declared himself "the way" and "the truth," but also "the life." God is Life; and as there is but one God, there can be but one Life. Must man die, then, in order to inherit eternal life and enter heaven?

Our Master said, "The kingdom of heaven is at hand." Then God and heaven, or Life, are present, and death is not the real stepping-stone to Life and happiness. They are now and here; and a change in human consciousness, from sin to holiness, would reveal this wonder of being. Because God is ever present, no boundary of time can separate us from Him and the heaven of His presence; and because God is Life, all Life is eternal.

Is it unchristian to believe there is no death? Not unless it be a sin to believe that God is Life and All-in-all. Evil and disease do not testify of Life and God.

Human beings are physically mortal, but spiritually immortal. The evil accompanying physical personality is illusive and mortal; but the good attendant upon spiritual individuality is immortal. Existing here and now, this unseen individuality is real and eternal. The so-called material senses, and the mortal mind which is misnamed man, take no cognizance of spiritual individuality, which manifests immortality, whose Principle is God.

To God alone belong the indisputable realities of being. Death is a contradiction of Life, or God; therefore it is not in accordance with His law, but antagonistic thereto.

Death, then, is error, opposed to Truth,—even the unreality of mortal mind, not the reality of that Mind which is Life. Error has no life, and is virtually without existence. Life is real; and all is real which proceeds from Life and is inseparable from it.

It is unchristian to believe in the transition called material death, since matter has no life, and such misbelief must enthrone another power, an imaginary life, above the living and true God. A material sense of life robs God, by declaring that not He alone is Life, but that something else also is life,—thus affirming the existence and rulership of more gods than one. This idolatrous and false sense of life is all that dies, or appears to die.

The opposite understanding of God brings to light Life and immortality. Death has no quality of Life; and no divine fiat commands us to believe in aught which is unlike God, or to deny that He is Life eternal.

Life as God, moral and spiritual good, is not seen in the mineral, vegetable, or animal kingdoms. Hence the inevitable conclusion that Life is not in these kingdoms, and that the popular views to this effect are not up to the Christian standard of Life, or equal to the reality of being, whose Principle is God.

When "the Word" is "made flesh" among mortals, the Truth of Life is rendered practical on the body. Eternal Life is partially understood; and sickness, sin, and death yield to holiness, health, and Life,—that is, to God. The lust of the flesh and the pride of physical life must be quenched in the divine essence,—that omnipotent Love which annihilates hate, that Life which knows no death.

"Who hath believed our report?" Who understands these sayings? He to whom the arm of the Lord is revealed. He loves them from whom divine Science removes human weakness by divine strength, and who unveil the Messiah, whose name is Wonderful.

Man has no underived power. That selfhood is false which opposes itself to God, claims another father, and denies spiritual sonship; but as many as receive the knowledge of God in Science must reflect, in some degree, the power of Him who gave and giveth man dominion over all the earth.

As soldiers of the cross we must be brave, and let Science declare the immortal status of man, and deny the evidence of the material senses, which testify that man dies.

As the image of God, or Life, man forever reflects and embodies Life, not death. The material senses testify falsely. They presuppose that God is good and that man is evil, that Deity is deathless, but that man dies, losing the divine likeness.

Science and material sense conflict at all points, from the revolution of the earth to the fall of a sparrow. It is mortality only that dies.

To say that you and I, as mortals, will not enter this dark shadow of material sense, called death, is to assert what we have not proved; but man in Science never dies. Material sense, or the belief of life in matter, must perish, in order to prove man deathless.

As Truth supersedes error, and bears the fruits of Love, this understanding of Truth subordinates the belief in death, and demonstrates Life as imperative in the divine order of being.

Jesus declares that they who believe his sayings will never die; therefore mortals can no more receive everlasting life by believing in death, than they can become perfect by believing in imperfection and living imperfectly.

Life is God, and God is good. Hence Life abides in man, if man abides in good, if he lives in God, who holds Life by a spiritual and not by a material sense of being.

A sense of death is not requisite to a proper or true sense of Life, but beclouds it. Death can never alarm or even appear to him who fully understands Life. The death-penalty comes through our ignorance of Life,—of that which is without beginning and without end,—and is the punishment of this ignorance.

Holding a material sense of Life, and lacking the spiritual sense of it, mortals die, in belief, and regard all things as temporal. A sense material apprehends nothing strictly belonging to the nature and office of Life. It conceives and beholds nothing but mortality, and has but a feeble concept of immortality.

In order to reach the true knowledge and consciousness of Life, we must learn it of good. Of evil we can never learn it, because sin shuts out the real sense of Life, and brings in an unreal sense of suffering and death.

Knowledge of evil, or belief in it, involves a loss of the true sense of good, God; and to know death, or to believe in it, involves a temporary loss of God, the infinite and only Life.

Resurrection from the dead (that is, from the belief in death) must come to all sooner or later; and they who have part in this resurrection are they upon whom the second death has no power.

The sweet and sacred sense of the permanence of man's unity with his Maker can illumine our present being with a continual presence and power of good, opening wide the portal from death into Life; and when this Life shall appear "we shall be like Him," and we shall go to the Father, not through death, but through Life; not through error, but through Truth.

All Life is Spirit, and Spirit can never dwell in its antagonist, matter. Life, therefore, is deathless, because God cannot be the opposite of Himself. In Christian Science there is no matter; hence matter neither lives nor dies. To the senses, matter appears to both live and die, and these phenomena appear to go on ad infinitum; but such a theory implies perpetual disagreement with Spirit.

Life, God, being everywhere, it must follow that death can be nowhere; because there is no place left for it.

Soul, Spirit, is deathless. Matter, sin, and death are not the outcome of Spirit, holiness, and Life. What then are matter, sin, and death? They can be nothing except the results of material consciousness; but material consciousness can have no real existence, because it is not a living—that is to say, a divine and intelligent—reality.

That man must be vicious before he can be virtuous, dying before he can be deathless, material before he can be spiritual, is an error of the senses; for the very opposite of this error is the genuine Science of being.

Man, in Science, is as perfect and immortal now, as when "the morning stars sang together, and all the sons of God shouted for joy."

With Christ, Life was not merely a sense of existence, but a sense of might and ability to subdue material conditions. No wonder "people were astonished at his doctrine; for he taught them as one having authority, and not as the scribes."

As defined by Jesus, Life had no beginning; nor was it the result of organization, or of an infusion of power into matter. To him, Life was Spirit.

Truth, defiant of error or matter, is Science, dispelling a false sense and leading man into the true sense of selfhood and Godhood; wherein the mortal does not develop the immortal, nor the material the spiritual, but wherein true manhood and womanhood go forth in the radiance of eternal being and its perfections, unchanged and unchangeable.

This generation seems too material for any strong demonstration over death, and hence cannot bring out the infinite reality of Life,—namely, that there is no death, but only Life. The present mortal sense of being is too finite for anchorage in infinite good, God, because mortals now believe in the possibility that Life can be evil.

The achievement of this ultimatum of Science, complete triumph over death, requires time and immense spiritual growth.

I have by no means spoken of myself, I cannot speak of myself as "sufficient for these things." I insist only upon the fact, as it exists in divine Science, that man dies not, and on the words of the Master in support of this verity,— words which can never "pass away till all be fulfilled."

Because of these profound reasons I urge Christians to have more faith in living than in dying. I exhort them to accept Christ's promise, and unite the influence of their own thoughts with the power of his teachings, in the Science of being. This will interpret the divine power to human capacity, and enable us to apprehend, or lay hold upon, "that for which," as Paul says in the third chapter of Philippians, we are also "apprehended of [or grasped by] Christ Jesus,"—the ever-present Life which knows no death, the omnipresent Spirit which knows no matter.

Personal Statements

Many misrepresentations are made concerning my
doctrines, some of which are as unkind and unjust as they
are untrue; but I can only repeat the Master's words: "They
know not what they do."

The foundations of these assertions, like the structure
raised thereupon, are vain shadows, repeating—if the
popular couplet may be so paraphrased—

The old, old story,

Of Satan and his lie.

In the days of Eden, humanity was misled by a false
personality,—a talking snake,—according to Biblical
history. This pretender taught the opposite of Truth. This
abortive ego, this fable of error, is laid bare in Christian
Science.

Human theories call, or miscall, this evil a child of God.
Philosophy would multiply and subdivide personality into
everything that exists, whether expressive or not expressive
of the Mind which is God. Human wisdom says of evil,
"The Lord knows it!" thus carrying out the serpent's
assurance: "In the day ye eat thereof [when you, lie, get the
floor], then your eyes shall be opened [you shall be
conscious matter], and ye shall be as gods, knowing good
and evil [you shall believe a lie, and this lie shall seem
truth]."

Bruise the head of this serpent, as Truth and "the woman" are doing in Christian Science, and it stings your heel, rears its crest proudly, and goes on saying, "Am I not myself? Am I not mind and matter, person and thing?" We should answer: "Yes! you are indeed yourself, and need most of all to be rid of this self, for it is very far from God's likeness."

The egotist must come down and learn, in humility, that God never made evil. An evil ego, and his assumed power, are falsities. These falsities need a denial. The falsity is the teaching that matter can be conscious; and conscious matter implies pantheism. This pantheism I unveil. I try to show its all-pervading presence in certain forms of theology and philosophy, where it becomes error's affirmative to Truth's negative. Anatomy and physiology make mind-matter a habitant of the cerebellum, whence it telegraphs and telephones over its own body, and goes forth into an imaginary sphere of its own creation and limitation, until it finally dies in order to better itself. But Truth never dies, and death is not the goal which Truth seeks.

The evil ego has but the visionary substance of matter. It lacks the substance of Spirit,—Mind, Life, Soul. Mortal mind is self-creative and self-sustained, until it becomes non-existent. It has no origin or existence in Spirit, immortal Mind, or good. Matter is not truly conscious; and mortal error, called mind, is not Godlike. These are the shadowy and false, which neither think nor speak.

All Truth is from inspiration and revelation,—from Spirit, not from flesh.

We do not see much of the real man here, for he is God's man; while ours is man's man.

I do not deny, I maintain, the individuality and reality of man; but I do so on a divine Principle, not based on a human conception and birth. The scientific man and his Maker are here; and you would be none other than this man, if you would subordinate the fleshly perceptions to the spiritual sense and source of being.

Jesus said, "I and my Father are one." He taught no selfhood as existent in matter. In his identity there is no evil. Individuality and Life were real to him only as spiritual and good, not as material or evil. This incensed the rabbins against Jesus, because it was an indignity to their personality; and this personality they regarded as both good and evil, as is still claimed by the worldly-wise. To them evil was even more the ego than was the good. Sin, sickness, and death were evil's concomitants. This evil ego they believed must extend throughout the universe, as being equally identical and self-conscious with God. This ego was in the earthquake, thunderbolt, and tempest.

The Pharisees fought Jesus on this issue. It furnished the battle-ground of the past, as it does of the present. The fight was an effort to enthrone evil. Jesus assumed the burden of disproof by destroying sin, sickness, and death, to sight and sense.

Nowhere in Scripture is evil connected with good, the being of God, and with every passing hour it is losing its false claim to existence or consciousness. All that can exist is God and His idea.

Credo

It is fair to ask of every one a reason for the faith within.
Though it be but to repeat my twice-told tale,—nay, the
tale already told a hundred times,—yet ask, and I will
answer.

Do you believe in God?

I believe more in Him than do most Christians, for I have
no faith in any other thing or being. He sustains my
individuality. Nay, more—He is my individuality and my
Life. Because He lives, I live. He heals all my ills, destroys
my iniquities, deprives death of its sting, and robs the grave
of its victory.

To me God is All. He is best understood as Supreme Being,
as infinite and conscious Life, as the affectionate Father
and Mother of all He creates; but this divine Parent no
more enters into His creation than the human father enters
into his child. His creation is not the Ego, but the reflection
of the Ego. The Ego is God Himself, the infinite Soul.

I believe that of which I am conscious through the
understanding, however faintly able to demonstrate Truth
and Love.

Do you believe in man?

I believe in the individual man, for I understand that man is as definite and eternal as God, and that man is coexistent with God, as being the eternally divine idea. This is demonstrable by the simple appeal to human consciousness.

But I believe less in the sinner, wrongly named man. The more I understand true humanhood, the more I see it to be sinless,—as ignorant of sin as is the perfect Maker.

To me the reality and substance of being are good, and nothing else. Through the eternal reality of existence I reach, in thought, a glorified consciousness of the only living God and the genuine man. So long as I hold evil in consciousness, I cannot be wholly good.

You cannot simultaneously serve the mammon of materiality and the God of spirituality. There are not two realities of being, two opposite states of existence. One should appear real to us, and the other unreal, or we lose the Science of being. Standing in no basic Truth, we make "the worse appear the better reason," and the unreal masquerades as the real, in our thought.

Evil is without Principle. Being destitute of Principle, it is devoid of Science. Hence it is undemonstrable, without proof. This gives me a clearer right to call evil a negation, than to affirm it to be something which God sees and knows, but which He straightway commands mortals to shun or relinquish, lest it destroy them. This notion of the destructibility of Mind implies the possibility of its defilement; but how can infinite Mind be defiled?

Do you believe in matter?

I believe in matter only as I believe in evil, that it is something to be denied and destroyed to human consciousness, and is unknown to the Divine. We should watch and pray that we enter not into the temptation of pantheistic belief in matter as sensible mind. We should subjugate it as Jesus did, by a dominant understanding of Spirit.

At best, matter is only a phenomenon of mortal mind, of which evil is the highest degree; but really there is no such thing as mortal mind,—though we are compelled to use the phrase in the endeavor to express the underlying thought.

In reality there are no material states or stages of consciousness, and matter has neither Mind nor sensation. Like evil, it is destitute of Mind, for Mind is God.

The less consciousness of evil or matter mortals have, the easier it is for them to evade sin, sickness, and death,— which are but states of false belief,—and awake from the troubled dream, a consciousness which is without Mind or Maker.

Matter and evil cannot be conscious, and consciousness should not be evil. Adopt this rule of Science, and you will discover the material origin, growth, maturity, and death of sinners, as the history of man, disappears, and the everlasting facts of being appear, wherein man is the reflection of immutable good.

Reasoning from false premises,—that Life is material, that immortal Soul is sinful, and hence that sin is eternal,—the reality of being is neither seen, felt, heard, nor understood. Human philosophy and human reason can never make one hair white or black, except in belief; whereas the demonstration of God, as in Christian Science, is gained through Christ as perfect manhood.

In pantheism the world is bereft of its God, whose place is ill supplied by the pretentious usurpation, by matter, of the heavenly sovereignty.

What say you of woman?

Man is the generic term for all humanity. Woman is the highest species of man, and this word is the generic term for all women; but not one of all these individualities is an Eve or an Adam. They have none of them lost their harmonious state, in the economy of God's wisdom and government.

The Ego is divine consciousness, eternally radiating throughout all space in the idea of God, good, and not of His opposite, evil. The Ego is revealed as Father, Son, and Holy Ghost; but the full Truth is found only in divine Science, where we see God as Life, Truth, and Love. In the scientific relation of man to God, man is reflected not as human soul, but as the divine ideal, whose Soul is not in body, but is God,—the divine Principle of man. Hence Soul is sinless and immortal, in contradistinction to the supposition that there can be sinful souls or immortal sinners.

This Science of God and man is the Holy Ghost, which reveals and sustains the unbroken and eternal harmony of both God and the universe. It is the kingdom of heaven, the ever-present reign of harmony, already with us. Hence the need that human consciousness should become divine, in the coincidence of God and man, in contradistinction to the false consciousness of both good and evil, God and devil,—of man separated from his Maker. This is the precious redemption of soul, as mortal sense, through Christ's immortal sense of Truth, which presents Truth's spiritual idea, man and woman.

What say you of evil?

God is not the so-called ego of evil; for evil, as a supposition, is the father of itself,—of the material world, the flesh, and the devil. From this falsehood arise the self-destroying elements of this world, its unkind forces, its tempests, lightnings, earthquakes, poisons, rabid beasts, fatal reptiles, and mortals.

Why are earth and mortals so elaborate in beauty, color, and form, if God has no part in them? By the law of opposites. The most beautiful blossom is often poisonous, and the most beautiful mansion is sometimes the home of vice. The senses, not God, Soul, form the condition of beautiful evil, and the supposed modes of self-conscious matter, which make a beautiful lie. Now a lie takes its pattern from Truth, by reversing Truth. So evil and all its forms are inverted good. God never made them; but the lie must say He made them, or it would not be evil. Being a lie, it would be truthful to call itself a lie; and by calling the knowledge of evil good, and greatly to be desired, it constitutes the lie an evil.

The reality and individuality of man are good and God-made, and they are here to be seen and demonstrated; it is only the evil belief that renders them obscure.

Matter and evil are anti-Christian, the antipodes of Science. To say that Mind is material, or that evil is Mind, is a misapprehension of being,—a mistake which will die of its own delusion; for being self-contradictory, it is also self-destructive. The harmony of man's being is not built on such false foundations, which are no more logical, philosophical, or scientific than would be the assertion that the rule of addition is the rule of subtraction, and that sums done under both rules would have one quotient.

Man's individuality is not a mortal mind or sinner; or else he has lost his true individuality as a perfect child of God. Man's Father is not a mortal mind and a sinner; or else the immortal and unerring Mind, God, is not his Father; but God is man's origin and loving Father, hence that saying of Jesus, "Call no man your father upon the earth: for one is your Father, which is in heaven."

The bright gold of Truth is dimmed by the doctrine of mind in matter.

To say there is a false claim, called sickness, is to admit all there is of sickness; for it is nothing but a false claim. To be healed, one must lose sight of a false claim. If the claim be present to the thought, then disease becomes as tangible as any reality. To regard sickness as a false claim, is to abate the fear of it; but this does not destroy the so-called fact of the claim. In order to be whole, we must be insensible to every claim of error.

As with sickness, so is it with sin. To admit that sin has any claim whatever, just or unjust, is to admit a dangerous fact. Hence the fact must be denied; for if sin's claim be allowed in any degree, then sin destroys the at-one-ment, or oneness with God,—a unity which sin recognizes as its most potent and deadly enemy.

If God knows sin, even as a false claimant, then acquaintance with that claimant becomes legitimate to mortals, and this knowledge would not be forbidden; but God forbade man to know evil at the very beginning, when Satan held it up before man as something desirable and a distinct addition to human wisdom, because the knowledge of evil would make man a god,—a representation that God both knew and admitted the dignity of evil.

Which is right,—God, who condemned the knowledge of sin and disowned its acquaintance, or the serpent, who pushed that claim with the glittering audacity of diabolical and sinuous logic?

Suffering from Others' Thoughts

Jesus accepted the one fact whereby alone the rule of Life can be demonstrated,—namely, that there is no death.

In his real self he bore no infirmities. Though "a man of sorrows, and acquainted with grief," as Isaiah says of him, he bore not his sins, but ours, "in his own body on the tree." "He was bruised for our iniquities; ... and with his stripes we are healed."

He was the Way-shower; and Christian Scientists who would demonstrate "the way" must keep close to his path, that they may win the prize. "The way," in the flesh, is the suffering which leads out of the flesh. "The way," in Spirit, is "the way" of Life, Truth, and Love, redeeming us from the false sense of the flesh and the wounds it bears. This threefold Messiah reveals the self-destroying ways of error and the life-giving way of Truth.

Job's faith and hope gained him the assurance that the so-called sufferings of the flesh are unreal. We shall learn how false are the pleasures and pains of material sense, and behold the truth of being, as expressed in his conviction, "Yet in my flesh shall I see God;" that is, Now and here shall I behold God, divine Love.

The chaos of mortal mind is made the stepping-stone to the cosmos of immortal Mind.

If Jesus suffered, as the Scriptures declare, it must have been from the mentality of others; since all suffering comes from mind, not from matter, and there could be no sin or suffering in the Mind which is God. Not his own sins, but the sins of the world, "crucified the Lord of glory," and "put him to an open shame."

Holding a quickened sense of false environment, and suffering from mentality in opposition to Truth, are significant of that state of mind which the actual understanding of Christian Science first eliminates and then destroys.

In the divine order of Science every follower of Christ shares his cup of sorrows. He also suffereth in the flesh, and from the mentality which opposes the law of Spirit; but the divine law is supreme, for it freeth him from the law of sin and death.

Prophets and apostles suffered from the thoughts of others. Their conscious being was not fully exempt from physicality and the sense of sin.

Until he awakes from his delusion, he suffers least from sin who is a hardened sinner. The hypocrite's affections must first be made to fret in their chains; and the pangs of hell must lay hold of him ere he can change from flesh to Spirit, become acquainted with that Love which is without dissimulation and endureth all things. Such mental conditions as ingratitude, lust, malice, hate, constitute the miasma of earth. More obnoxious than Chinese stenchpots are these dispositions which offend the spiritual sense.

Anatomically considered, the design of the material senses is to warn mortals of the approach of danger by the pain they feel and occasion; but as this sense disappears it foresees the impending doom and foretells the pain. Man's refuge is in spirituality, "under the shadow of the Almighty."

The cross is the central emblem of human history. Without it there is neither temptation nor glory. When Jesus turned and said, "Who hath touched me?" he must have felt the influence of the woman's thought; for it is written that he felt that "virtue had gone out of him." His pure consciousness was discriminating, and rendered this infallible verdict; but he neither held her error by affinity nor by infirmity, for it was detected and dismissed.

This gospel of suffering brought life and bliss. This is earth's Bethel in stone,—its pillow, supporting the ladder which reaches heaven.

Suffering was the confirmation of Paul's faith. Through "a thorn in the flesh" he learned that spiritual grace was sufficient for him.

Peter rejoiced that he was found worthy to suffer for Christ; because to suffer with him is to reign with him.

Sorrow is the harbinger of joy. Mortal throes of anguish forward the birth of immortal being; but divine Science wipes away all tears.

The only conscious existence in the flesh is error of some sort,—sin, pain, death,—a false sense of life and happiness. Mortals, if at ease in so-called existence, are in their native element of error, and must become dis-eased, dis-quieted, before error is annihilated.

Jesus walked with bleeding feet the thorny earth-road, treading "the winepress alone." His persecutors said mockingly, "Save thyself, and come down from the cross." This was the very thing he was doing, coming down from the cross, saving himself after the manner that he had taught, by the law of Spirit's supremacy; and this was done through what is humanly called agony.

Even the ice-bound hypocrite melts in fervent heat, before he apprehends Christ as "the way." The Master's sublime triumph over all mortal mentality was immortality's goal. He was too wise not to be willing to test the full compass of human woe, being "in all points tempted like as we are, yet without sin."

Thus the absolute unreality of sin, sickness, and death was revealed,—a revelation that beams on mortal sense as the midnight sun shines over the Polar Sea.

The Saviour's Mission

If there is no reality in evil, why did the Messiah come to the world, and from what evils was it his purpose to save humankind? How, indeed, is he a Saviour, if the evils from which he saves are nonentities?

Jesus came to earth; but the Christ (that is, the divine idea of the divine Principle which made heaven and earth) was never absent from the earth and heaven; hence the phraseology of Jesus, who spoke of the Christ as one who came down from heaven, yet as "the Son of man which is in heaven." (John iii. 13.) By this we understand Christ to be the divine idea brought to the flesh in the son of Mary.

Salvation is as eternal as God. To mortal thought Jesus appeared as a child, and grew to manhood, to suffer before Pilate and on Calvary, because he could reach and teach mankind only through this conformity to mortal conditions;

but Soul never saw the Saviour come and go, because the divine idea is always present.

Jesus came to rescue men from these very illusions to which he seemed to conform: from the illusion which calls sin real, and man a sinner, needing a Saviour; the illusion which calls sickness real, and man an invalid, needing a physician; the illusion that death is as real as Life. From such thoughts—mortal inventions, one and all—Christ Jesus came to save men, through ever-present and eternal good.

Mortal man is a kingdom divided against itself. With the same breath he articulates truth and error. We say that God is All, and there is none beside Him, and then talk of sin and sinners as real. We call God omnipotent and omnipresent, and then conjure up, from the dark abyss of nothingness, a powerful presence named evil. We say that harmony is real, and inharmony is its opposite, and therefore unreal; yet we descant upon sickness, sin, and death as realities.

With the tongue "bless we God, even the Father; and therewith curse we men, who are made after the similitude [human concept] of God. Out of the same mouth proceedeth blessing and cursing. My brethren, these things ought not so to be." (James iii. 9, 10.) Mortals are free moral agents, to choose whom they would serve. If God, then let them serve Him, and He will be unto them All-in-all.

If God is ever present, He is neither absent from Himself nor from the universe. Without Him, the universe would disappear, and space, substance, and immortality be lost. St. Paul says, "And if Christ be not raised, your faith is vain; ye are yet in your sins." (1 Corinthians xv. 17.) Christ cannot come to mortal and material sense, which sees not God. This false sense of substance must yield to His eternal presence, and so dissolve. Rising above the false, to the true evidence of Life, is the resurrection that takes hold of eternal Truth. Coming and going belong to mortal consciousness. God is "the same yesterday, and to-day, and forever."

To material sense, Jesus first appeared as a helpless human babe; but to immortal and spiritual vision he was one with the Father, even the eternal idea of God, that was—and is—neither young nor old, neither dead nor risen. The mutations of mortal sense are the evening and the morning of human thought,—the twilight and dawn of earthly vision, which precedeth the nightless radiance of divine Life. Human perception, advancing toward the apprehension of its nothingness, halts, retreats, and again goes forward; but the divine Principle and Spirit and spiritual man are unchangeable,—neither advancing, retreating, nor halting.

Our highest sense of infinite good in this mortal sphere is but the sign and symbol, not the substance of good. Only faith and a feeble understanding make the earthly acme of human sense. "The life which I now live in the flesh I live by the faith of the Son of God." (Galatians ii. 20.)

Christian Science is both demonstration and fruition, but how attenuated are our demonstration and realization of this Science! Truth, in divine Science, is the stepping-stone to the understanding of God; but the broken and contrite heart soonest discerns this truth, even as the helpless sick are soonest healed by it. Invalids say, "I have recovered from sickness;" when the fact really remains, in divine Science, that they never were sick.

The Christian saith, "Christ (God) died for me, and came to save me;" yet God dies not, and is the ever-presence that neither comes nor goes, and man is forever His image and likeness. "The things which are seen are temporal; but the things which are not seen are eternal." (2 Corinthians iv. 18.) This is the mystery of godliness—that God, good, is never absent, and there is none beside good. Mortals can understand this only as they reach the Life of good, and learn that there is no Life in evil. Then shall it appear that the true ideal of omnipotent and ever-present good is an ideal wherein and wherefor there is no evil. Sin exists only as a sense, and not as Soul. Destroy this sense of sin, and sin disappears. Sickness, sin, or death is a false sense of Life and good. Destroy this trinity of error, and you find Truth.

In Science, Christ never died. In material sense Jesus died, and lived. The fleshly Jesus seemed to die, though he did not. The Truth or Life in divine Science—undisturbed by human error, sin, and death—saith forever, "I am the living God, and man is My idea, never in matter, nor resurrected from it." "Why seek ye the living among the dead? He is not here, but is risen." (Luke xxiv. 5, 6.) Mortal sense, confining itself to matter, is all that can be buried or resurrected.

Mary had risen to discern faintly God's ever-presence, and that of His idea, man; but her mortal sense, reversing Science and spiritual understanding, interpreted this appearing as a risen Christ. The I am was neither buried nor resurrected. The Way, the Truth, and the Life were never absent for a moment. This trinity of Love lives and reigns forever. Its kingdom, not apparent to material sense, never disappeared to spiritual sense, but remained forever in the Science of being. The so-called appearing, disappearing, and reappearing of ever-presence, in whom is no variableness or shadow of turning, is the false human sense of that light which shineth in darkness, and the darkness comprehendeth it not.

Summary

All that is, God created. If sin has any pretense of existence, God is responsible therefor; but there is no reality in sin, for God can no more behold it, or acknowledge it, than the sun can coexist with darkness.

To build the individual spiritual sense, conscious of only health, holiness, and heaven, on the foundations of an eternal Mind which is conscious of sickness, sin, and death, is a moral impossibility; for "other foundation can no man lay than that is laid." (1 Corinthians iii. 11.) The nearer we approximate to such a Mind, even if it were (or could be) God, the more real those mind-pictures would become to us; until the hope of ever eluding their dread presence must yield to despair, and the haunting sense of evil forever accompany our being.

Mortals may climb the smooth glaciers, leap the dark fissures, scale the treacherous ice, and stand on the summit of Mont Blanc; but they can never turn back what Deity knoweth, nor escape from identification with what dwelleth in the eternal Mind.

74705807R00035

Made in the USA
Middletown, DE
29 May 2018